YOU SHOULD MEET
Mae Jemison

by Laurie Calkhoven
illustrated by Monique Dong

Ready-to-Read

Simon Spotlight
New York   London   Toronto   Sydney   New Delhi

SIMON SPOTLIGHT

An imprint of Simon & Schuster Children's Publishing Division

1230 Avenue of the Americas, New York, New York 10020

This Simon Spotlight edition September 2016

For information about special discounts for bulk purchases, please contact Simon & Schuster Special Sales at
1-866-506-1949 or business@simonandschuster.com.

Manufactured in the United States of America 0716 LAK

2 4 6 8 10 9 7 5 3 1

Library of Congress Cataloging-in-Publication Data:

Names: Calkhoven, Laurie. | Dong, Monique, illustrator.

Title: Mae Jemison / by Laurie Calkhoven; illustrated by Monique Dong.

Description: First edition. | New York: Simon Spotlight, 2016.

Series: You should meet | Series: Ready-to-read

"Simon Spotlight, an imprint of Simon & Schuster Children's Publishing Division"—Page 2. | Audience: Age 6-8.

Identifiers: LCCN 2016021575| ISBN 9781481476492 | ISBN 9781481476515 | ISBN 9781481476508

Subjects: LCSH: Jemison, Mae, 1956—Juvenile literature. | African American women
astronauts—Biography—Juvenile literature. | Astronauts—United States—Biography—Juvenile literature.

Classification: LCC TL789.85.J46 C35 2016 | DDC 629.450092 [B]—dc23 LC record available
at https://lccn.loc.gov/2016021575

CONTENTS

Have you ever looked up at the stars and wanted to fly? Have you dreamed of being an astronaut and blasting off into space? Or of being a dancer? Or being a doctor who brings medical care to people around the world?

If you've ever dreamed of any of those things, then you should meet Mae Jemison!

Mae is the first African American woman to become an astronaut. But she's much more than that. Mae is also . . .

a scientist

and a dancer.

And she's **a doctor, an author,**

and **a teacher.**
Today she's working to find ways for
humans to travel beyond our solar system.
Mae followed her dreams . . . all of them.
Once you meet her, you'll know you can
follow yours too!

Chapter 1
Early Dreams

Mae was born in Decatur, Alabama, on October 17, 1956. She has two older siblings, a sister and a brother. Her father was a carpenter and her mother taught elementary school.

When Mae was three years old, her family moved from Alabama to Chicago, Illinois. She thinks of Chicago as her hometown.

Mae always loved science. When her kindergarten teacher asked her what she wanted to be when she grew up, Mae said, "a scientist." Many people at the time didn't think it was possible for an African American girl to become a scientist. Women were more likely to become teachers and nurses than scientists.

"Don't you mean a nurse?" the teacher asked.

"No, I mean a **scientist**," Mae answered.

Other teachers tried to discourage Mae too. She wouldn't let them. She never stopped believing in herself. She stood strong in the face of other people's questions.

At home Mae was encouraged to be anything she wanted to be. "My parents were the best scientists I knew, because they were always asking questions," she said when she was grown up.

Mae considered herself a "busybody" and liked to get involved with her sister's and brother's science projects.

Once, she got a splinter in her thumb. Soon there was pus. Other kids might have been grossed out and just wanted it to go away, but not Mae. Mae wanted to know exactly what the pus was and where it came from. So she did a scientific study of pus to learn about how it fights infection to help our bodies heal.

Mae's family talked about many things around the dinner table, including the civil rights movement. The civil rights movement was a mass popular movement to secure equal access to and opportunities for the basic privileges and rights of US citizenship for African Americans. There were sometimes riots, and one time, National Guard soldiers came to Chicago to keep the peace. Mae was scared, but she promised herself that she wouldn't let fear keep her from doing what she wanted in the world.

The library was a place where Mae learned about science. She read all kinds of science books, especially ones about the stars.

Mae also followed the National Aeronautics and Space Administrations (NASA) space programs in the newspapers. She knew all about the astronauts and their missions.

"Growing up, I always assumed I would go into space," Mae said when she was older. "I remember being really, really irritated that there were no women astronauts."

Mae was inspired by the character Uhura, a female officer on the television show Star Trek. Uhura was played by the actress Nichelle Nichols. Eventually Mae got to meet Nichelle.

Mae believes that the best scientists are not only logical but creative too. She took all kinds of dance lessons growing up—ballet, jazz, modern, African, and even Japanese dancing. She wanted to be a professional dancer. She also designed and made clothes for her dolls, acted in school plays, and took art classes.

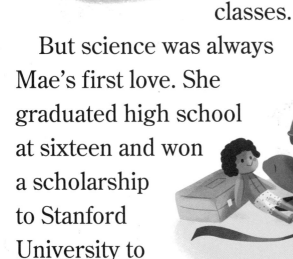

But science was always Mae's first love. She graduated high school at sixteen and won a scholarship to Stanford University to study engineering.

Chapter 2
Dreams on Earth

At Stanford University in California, Mae majored in chemical engineering. Biochemical engineering was her focus. A biochemical engineer creates things to make medical care better. Mae also majored in African and Afro-American history. And just like she had when she was younger, Mae combined art and creativity with science.

Mae created dance routines, acted in plays, and was president of the Black Student Union. She also learned to speak Swahili, an African language.

In college Mae decided that she wanted to be a medical doctor. When she graduated from Stanford, she moved to New York City to go to Cornell University Medical College. Mae studied hard, but she also made time for fun. She took dance lessons, and she went to the theater with friends.

During her summer breaks, Mae traveled to Kenya and Cuba to learn about medical care in other countries, especially for poor people.

She also worked in Thailand at a camp for *refugees*—people who had been driven away from their homes by war.

At first, Mae didn't want to be the kind of doctor who sees patients. She wanted to be the kind of doctor who does research. But working in other countries made her interested in bringing medicine to people in poor areas around the world.

After she became a doctor, Mae volunteered for the Peace Corps.

The Peace Corps is made up of Americans who bring things such as medical care, clean water, and education to people in underdeveloped countries. As a doctor for the Peace Corps, Mae went to Sierra Leone and Liberia, two countries in West Africa.

After two and a half years in Africa, Mae returned to California to work as a doctor. It was then that she remembered an early dream—a dream to fly into space.

She learned that NASA was accepting applications for the astronaut program, so Mae applied.

People who want to be astronauts must have college degrees in science, math, or engineering. They also need to have work experience in their fields and show NASA that they can be leaders.

Mae's application stood out. NASA asked her to travel to the Johnson Space Center in Houston, Texas, for interviews and physical tests. Mae must have shown them how smart and strong she was, because in June 1987 NASA asked her to be an astronaut candidate. She was one of fifteen chosen out of a group of two thousand people.

Mae's early dream was coming true. She was on her way to becoming an astronaut!

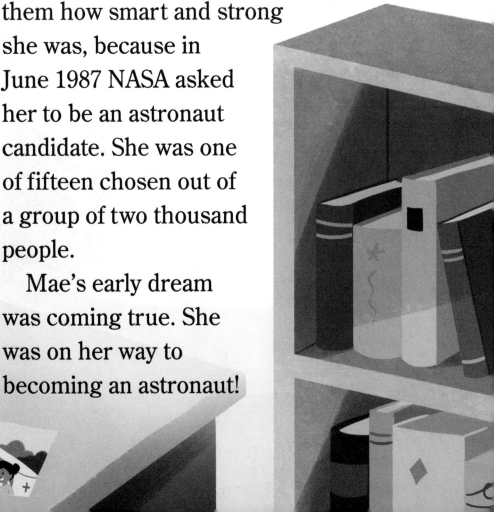

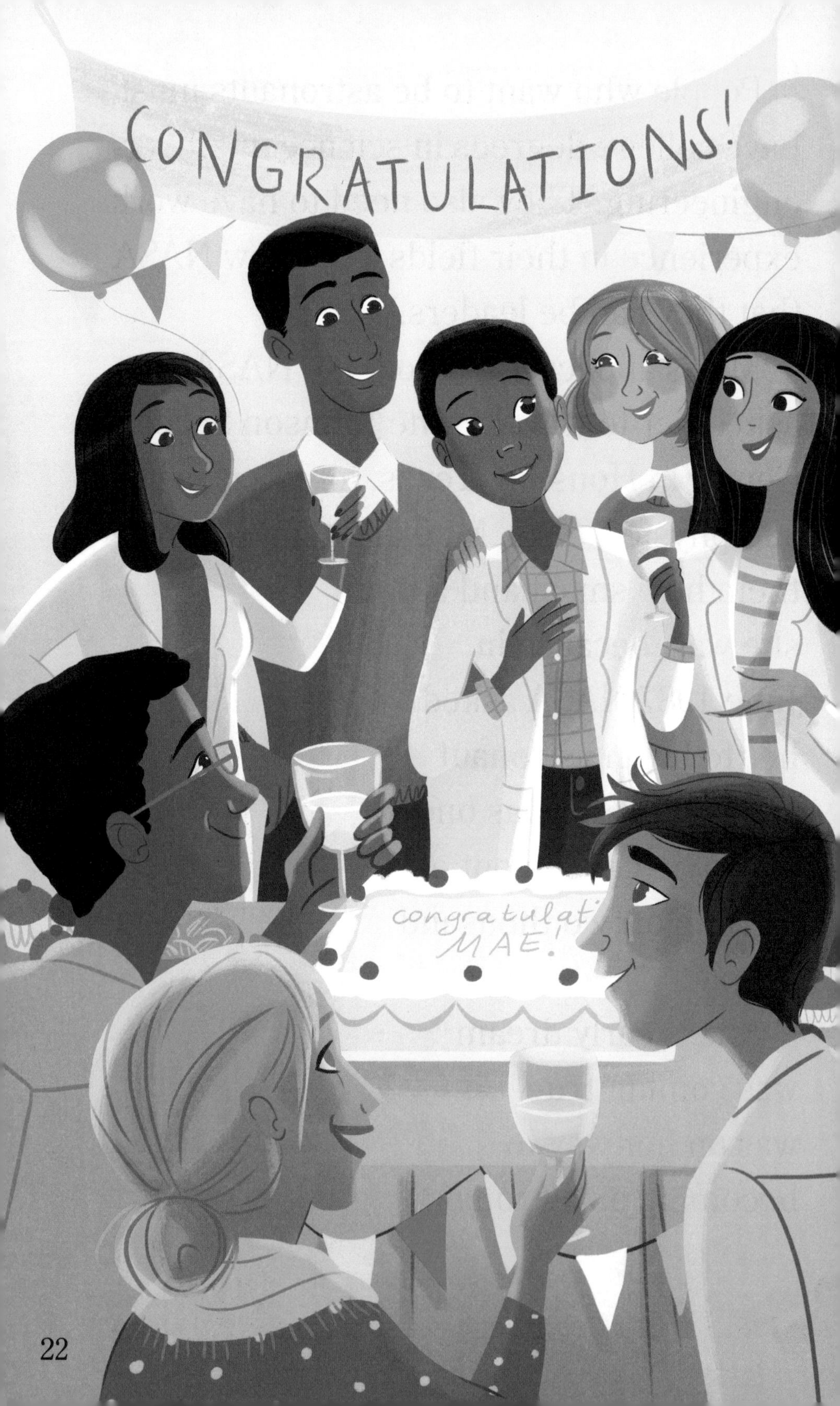
CONGRATULATIONS!
congratulat
MAE!

Chapter 3
Dreams about Space

Mae was chosen by NASA in 1987, but she wasn't an astronaut yet. She was an "astronaut *candidate*." A candidate is someone who is applying for a particular job. Astronaut candidates have to take classes and work hard to learn new things before they are given the title "astronaut."

One thing Mae had to learn before she could go into space was what it was like to be weightless. Astronauts call this *microgravity*. Gravity is the force that keeps humans—and everything else— from floating off Earth and into space. But in space you feel only a tiny amount of gravity's pull.

Astronauts need to be able to do their jobs while they are weightless. One way they learn how to do that is by flying in a special airplane. The plane makes many people sick to their stomachs.

The plane's nickname is the Vomit Comet!

Mae also needed to learn how to survive in the wilderness and in the water. That was in case her spaceship landed in the wrong place when it came back to Earth.

After a year of hard training, Mae was finally named an astronaut!

Not all astronauts fly into space. Many work on Earth, helping the astronauts who are in space. At first Mae worked as

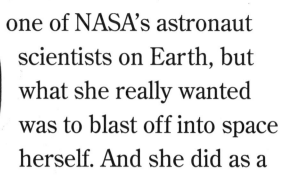

one of NASA's astronaut scientists on Earth, but what she really wanted was to blast off into space herself. And she did as a

Science Mission Specialist.

Science mission specialists perform experiments, among many other jobs, in space.

Chapter 4
Space!

On September 12, 1992, Mae became the first African American woman to travel into space.

The first white American woman to fly into space, Sally Ride, had done so in June 1983. The first African American male astronaut, Guion Bluford, had gone into space two months later in August 1983. Now Mae was making history by being both a woman and an African American.

Mae flew on the space shuttle *Endeavour*. She spent about eight days in space and completed almost 127 orbits of the Earth. In that time she traveled more than three million miles!

Mae wanted to celebrate art and creativity in space. Among other items, she brought a poster of an African American dancer and a statue made by a women's group in West Africa onto the shuttle.

In orbit, the astronauts did experiments. Mae wanted to know why some people get sick to their stomachs in space and how to make them feel better.

Mae also wanted to learn about how tadpoles grew when they were weightless. Mae discovered tadpoles grew just like they do in Earth's gravity.

"When we got back to Earth, the tadpoles were right on track," Mae told a reporter after her mission. The tadpoles later turned into frogs, just like they were supposed to.

Mae was never afraid in space. "I was very excited and happy," she said. She remembered being a young girl who loved to stare up at the stars.

"The first thing I saw from space was Chicago, my hometown. . . . Looking out the window of that space shuttle, I thought if that little girl growing up in Chicago could see her older self now, she would have a huge grin on her face."

The flight made Mae famous. She realized she could use her fame to talk about how important it is to take care of the planet. She also wanted people of all races to know they could be part of the scientific world.

Chapter 5
Life after Space

After flying into space, Mae decided to leave NASA and do other things. She became a college professor. She started a company that brings technology and better medical care to people in poor countries. She also became an actress when she appeared on the TV show *Star Trek: The Next Generation*. *Star Trek* was one of Mae's favorite TV shows when she was young.

Getting kids involved in science was also something Mae wanted to do. She started a camp for students who want to become scientists. The camp, called The Earth We Share, welcomes young scientists from all over the world.

These campers get to do more than hike or sleep in a tent. They use their imaginations and plan amazing things— such as a space mission to Mars!

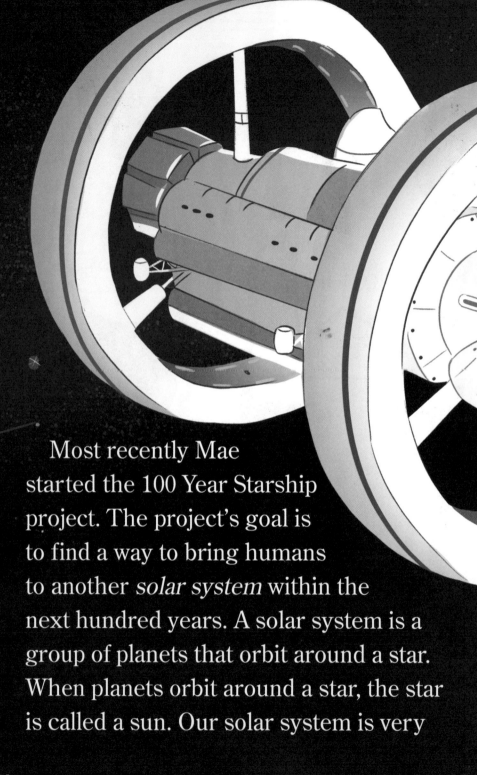

Most recently Mae
started the 100 Year Starship
project. The project's goal is
to find a way to bring humans
to another *solar system* within the
next hundred years. A solar system is a
group of planets that orbit around a star.
When planets orbit around a star, the star
is called a sun. Our solar system is very

far away from any other solar system.

Today it would take us seventy thousand years to travel to another solar system! The 100 Year Starship program will have to create everything from new kinds of energy to new kinds of filters that will keep air and water clean. A starship might need a garden for fresh fruits and vegetables, and things to help the astronauts survive on a new planet.

Most of all, Mae wants to make sure that all kinds of people, not just Americans and not just doctors, will have a chance to be involved.

Mae always believed in following her dreams, and she never let people tell her she couldn't. She also refused to become any one thing—a scientist or an artist, a doctor or a dancer. Mae believed she could do anything, and she did!

Now that you've met Mae Jemison, don't you think you can do the same thing? Reach for the stars—and more!

BUT WAIT . . .

THERE'S MORE!

Turn the page to try a science experiment similar to the ones Mae did in space, to read how Mae saved a life, and to read some facts about Mae's mission on board the space shuttle *Endeavour*.

Life Sciences Experiment

Aboard the space shuttle *Endeavour*, Mae did experiments to study how living things would react to being in space.

You can do experiments like Mae without even leaving your house! Follow the directions below to discover how plants react to three different environments.

Materials

3 plastic sandwich bags
12 dry pinto beans
3 paper towels
Water
Stapler with staples
Tape
Ruler
A journal or other place to write notes
A grown-up to help with the stapler

Step 1: Fold each paper towel into fourths so that it will fit into a sandwich bag.

Step 2: Put one folded paper towel into each bag.

Step 3: For each bag, staple four times through the paper towel, from right to left, about an inch from the bottom. Space out the staples evenly and make sure they are going straight across, not up and down.

Step 4: Inside the bag, place one bean on top of each staple.

Step 5: Find three different places to grow your beans, and tape one bag at each spot. Make sure each area has a different environment—someplace sunny, someplace shady, and someplace dark. Try taping one bag to a window, one to a wall beside a window, and another to the inside of a cabinet.

Step 6: Water your beans by pouring half an inch of water into each bag. Make sure the water doesn't rise above the staples.

Step 7: After about five days, you should see small green shoots sprouting from some of the beans.

Step 8: Keep watering your beans with half an inch of water once a week. Every time you water your plants, use the ruler to measure how long the shoots are, and then write down your findings. After a couple of weeks, you will start to notice a difference in the way the beans are growing.

Step 9: After two weeks, look at the measurements you've taken. Can you come to any conclusions about the way each environment affected the beans? Write your conclusions down.

Step 10: Now that you've made a discovery, share the results!

WHAT IT MEANS
This experiment studies how beans react to the amount of sunlight in their environment. You can study how beans react to other environments by changing the experiment. Make sure there is only one thing different about each environment for the beans. Otherwise, you won't know which change has affected the way they grow.

You can also experiment with:
• Different amounts of water.
• Different types of water, like salt water or sugar water.
• Different sources of light, like fluorescent or colored lightbulbs.
• Different temperatures.

Mae to the Rescue!

When Mae first became a doctor, she traveled to Sierra Leone in West Africa. She volunteered her medical services through the Peace Corps. Within two weeks one of the Peace Corps volunteers became very sick.

The other doctors thought the volunteer had malaria. Malaria is a disease that can cause a high fever, muscle pain, and vomiting. It is common in tropical climates like that of Sierra Leone. People can die of malaria if they are not treated. After receiving treatment for one day, the volunteer was worse. Mae knew that he did not have malaria. If he did not receive a different treatment, he would die.

Soon after the electricity went out at the hospital. Mae used a flashlight to search for medicine to give the volunteer a different treatment. Even if she found the medicine, it would not cure him completely. Mae was sure he was sick with meningitis. Meningitis is an illness that will kill a person if not treated correctly, and no one had the correct treatment nearby.

Mae ordered a military medical evacuation. That meant a plane would take the volunteer to an air force hospital for treatment. Mae was a new doctor, and she was giving an order that would cost more than eighty thousand dollars. The people at the US embassy did not think she could give such a big order.

Mae did not give up. She calmly explained that she had the power to give the order, and she clarified why it was absolutely necessary. She refused to take no for an answer—a man's life was at stake. The people at the embassy finally listened to her, and Mae evacuated with the volunteer. In all, she worked for fifty-six hours straight to save the man's life.

Thanks to Mae's self-confidence and brave decisions, the volunteer survived.

Mae's Mission by the Numbers

• Mae went into space on a mission called STS-47. It was the second flight of twenty-five for the space shuttle *Endeavour.*

• The mission lasted seven days, twenty-two hours, thirty minutes, twenty-three seconds from blast off to touchdown.

• The mission launched on September 12, 1992 at 10:23:00 a.m. Eastern Daylight Time and landed on September 20, 1992 at 8:53:23 a.m. Eastern Daylight Time.

• When the shuttle launched, it weighed 258,679 pounds. That's more than twenty-five school buses! When the shuttle landed, it weighed 218,854 pounds, having lost 39,825 pounds. Fuel, an external tank, and two solid rocket motors were either used up or ejected during the mission.

• The shuttle orbited Earth at an altitude, or height, of about 191 miles. That's about thirty-five times higher than the peak of Mount Everest.

• The shuttle orbited earth about 127 times, traveling 3.3 million miles. (That's close to the distance you'd travel to go to the moon and back seven times.)

• There were seven crew members.

• The STS-47 mission included three firsts: the first Japanese astronaut to fly aboard the shuttle, payload specialist Mamoru Mohri; the first African American woman to fly in space, mission specialist Mae Jemison; and the first married couple to fly on the same space expedition, mission specialists Mark C. Lee and N. Jan Davis.

Now that you've met Mae, what do you know about her?

1. What year was Mae born?

a. 1956   b. 1960   c. 1972

2. Mae believes that the best scientists are what?

a. Quiet   b. Curious   c. Stubborn

3. According to Mae, why were her parents the best scientists she knew?

a. They studied.   b. They day dreamed.   c. They asked questions.

4. Mae always knew she would do something specific. What was that?

a. Go to space   b. Be a leader   c. Study tadpoles

5. Besides science, what were some of Mae's interests?

a. Art and dance   b. Geography and history   c. Math and magic

6. When Mae finished medical school, what did she do next?

a. Started an organization   b. Joined the Peace Corps   c. Joined NASA

7. On September 12, 1992, Mae became the first ___ in space?

a. Woman   b. Doctor   c. African American woman

8. What did Mae do in space?

a. Conducted experiments   b. Built robots   c. Studied Earth

9. How did Mae feel in space?

a. Excited and afraid   b. Sick but happy   c. Excited and happy

10. After going to space, what did Mae want to do?

a. Help people and encourage space exploration.

b. Become a dancer and a writer.   c. Go on a mission to the sun.

Answers: 1.a 2.b 3.c 4.a 5.a 6.b 7.c 8.a 9.c 10.a